# First Prayers with School Friends

First Prayers with School Friends
By Cara Barilla

ISBN 9780645285161

Copyright Cara Barilla 2023
All rights reserved 2023

Published by Little Lemon Book Co.
SYDNEY
www.littlelemonbookco.com.au

Written by Cara Barilla
www.authorcarabarilla.com.au
◉ @AuthorCaraBarilla

Illustrated by Eleonora Cali
◉ @Roxanne_Drawings

Layout by Jessica Chaplin
www.jesschaplincreative.com.au
◉ @jesschaplincreative

This book is available in quantity for your group or organisation.
For more information please contact Little Lemon Book Co.

Printed in Australia.

No part of this publication may be reproduced in whole or in part,
or stored in a retrieval system or transmitted in any form or by any
means, electronic, mechanical, photocopying, recording or otherwise
without written permission of the publisher.

For preschool and primary school age.

Little Lemon Book Co. First Edition 2023

# First Prayers with School Friends

Written by Cara Barilla
Illustrated by Eleonora Cali

I thank the light

For showing me the way

And to shine so bright

for my friends to play

I thank God **always**
For giving me **cheer**
In the gloomiest of **days**
My friends are always **here**

May we rejoice
And celebrate pure light
Embracing gods choice
Living with pure sight

Let us **appreciate**

All the kindness at **reach**

Our teachers **illuminate**

With wisdom to **teach**

God give us strength

For a new tricky turn

For it is a growing length

That we all live to learn

Bless us Lord with *care*
To know when we can *be*
Open armed and always *there*
Supporting friends to help and *see*

Thanks to God for library *learning*
Library teachers share kind *insight*

God give us the courage
To shine out our inner voice
Our inner truth will encourage
To heal our friends and rejoice

And thank you God for my friends

They are a blessing to me

## About the Author

Cara Barilla is a proud mother of two children and resides in Sydney, Australia.

As an experienced writer and educator, she continues to use her passion of helping others through art and literature to find a piece of their happiness and one's connection of 'self love' through the powerful message of words.

Cara has a strong passion for art, creative writing, poetry, wellness and continues to inspire and assist people of all walks of life through her art of creativity.

www.ingramcontent.com/pod-product-compliance
Lightning Source LLC
Chambersburg PA
CBHW040731150426
42811CB00063B/1575